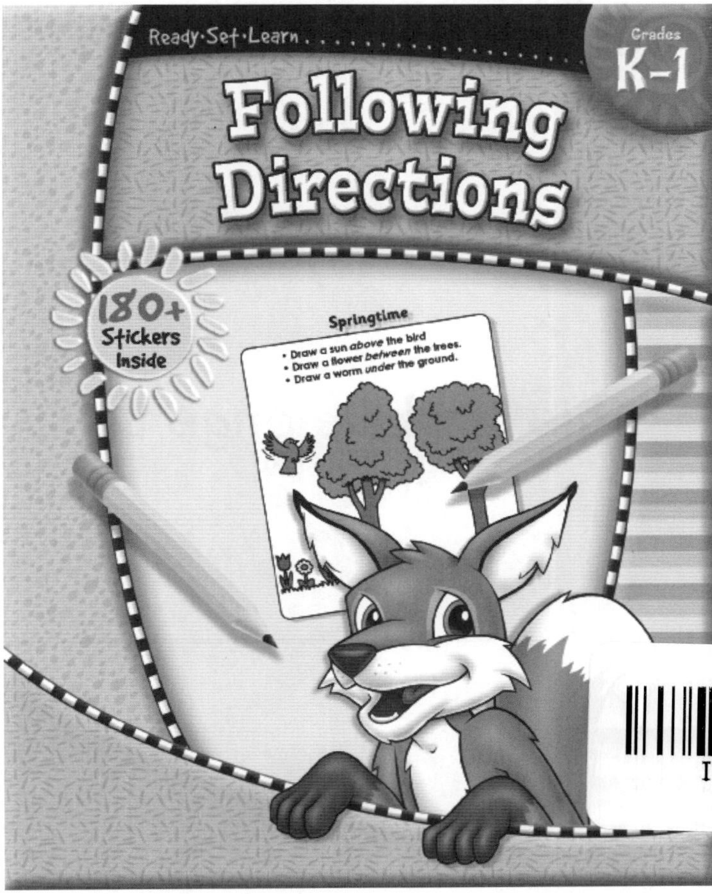

Managing Editor
Ina Massler Levin, M.A.

Editor
Eric Migliaccio

Contributing Editor
Sarah Smith

Creative Director
Karen J. Goldfluss, M.S. Ed.

Cover Design
Tony Carrillo / Marilyn Goldberg

Teacher Created Resources
12621 Western Avenue
Garden Grove, CA 92841
www.teachercreated.com

ISBN: 978-1-4206-5933-7

Reprinted, 2025 (PO606180)

Made in U.S.A.

This book belongs to

____

Ready·Set·Learn

Get Ready to Learn!

Get ready, get set, and go! Boost your child's learning with this exciting series of books. Geared to help children practice and master many needed skills, the *Ready·Set·Learn* books are bursting with 64 pages of learning fun. Use these books for . . .

- enrichment
- skills reinforcement
- extra practice

With their smaller size, the *Ready·Set·Learn* books fit easily in children's hands, backpacks, and book bags. All your child needs to get started are pencils, crayons, and colored pencils.

A full sheet of colorful stickers is included. Use these stickers for . . .

- decorating pages
- rewarding outstanding effort
- keeping track of completed pages

Celebrate your child's progress by using these stickers on the reward chart located on the inside cover. The blue-ribbon sticker fits perfectly on the certificate on page 64.

With *Ready·Set·Learn* and a little encouragement, your child will be on the fast track to learning fun!

From Bear to Ball

Directions:

1. Put your crayon on the teddy bear.
2. Draw a line from the teddy bear to the ball.
3. Color the flower.

Red Circles

Directions:

1. Trace and color the circles with a red crayon.
2. Trace and color the squares with a blue crayon.

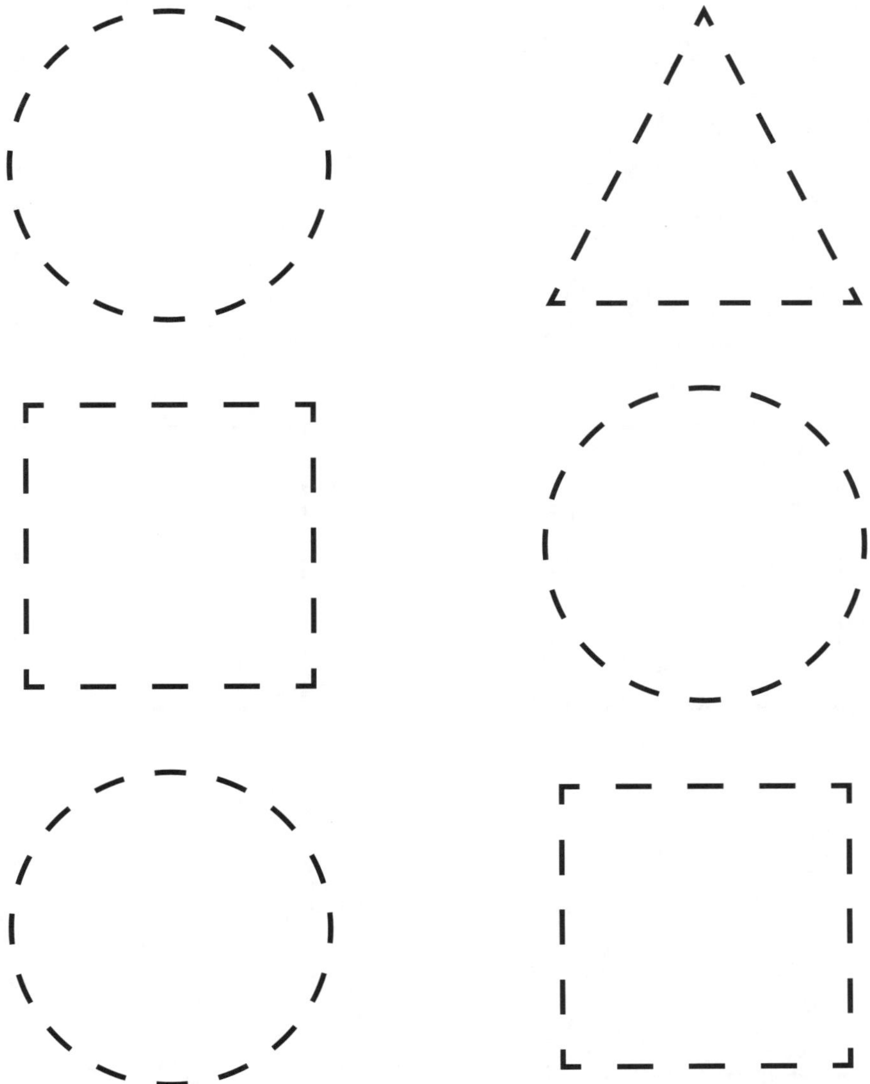

Yellow Triangles

Directions:

1. Trace and color the triangles with a yellow crayon.
2. Trace and color the squares with a green crayon.
3. Trace and color the circle with an orange crayon.

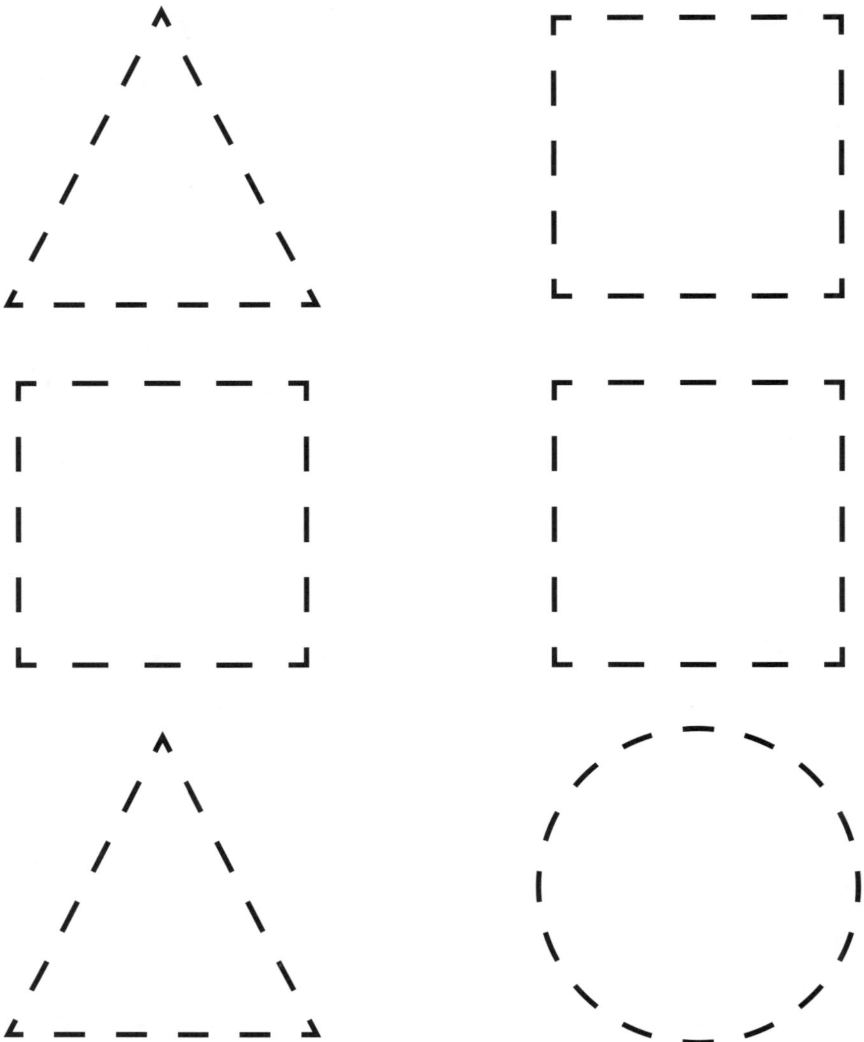

Green Fish

Directions:

1. Color the fish with a green crayon.
2. Make a ring around the duck.
3. Draw a line under the flower.

From B to b

Directions:

1. Draw a line to connect the uppercase *B* to the lowercase *b*.
2. Draw a line to connect the uppercase *K* to the lowercase *k*.

Y b B

s K d

k

C S

y D c

Box the Letters

Directions:

1. Use a blue crayon to draw a box around every uppercase or lowercase *a*.
2. Use a red crayon to draw a box around every uppercase or lowercase *t*.

A	r	T
w	Q	a
R	q	G
t	W	g

From Book to Bird

Directions:

1. Draw a line under the bird.
2. Make a triangle around the book.
3. Make an **X** on the sun.
4. Draw a line from the book to the bird.

Lots of Jars

Directions:

1. Cross out the jar of beads.
2. Draw a line under the jar of marbles.
3. Color the jar of pickles green.
4. Circle the jar of fireflies.

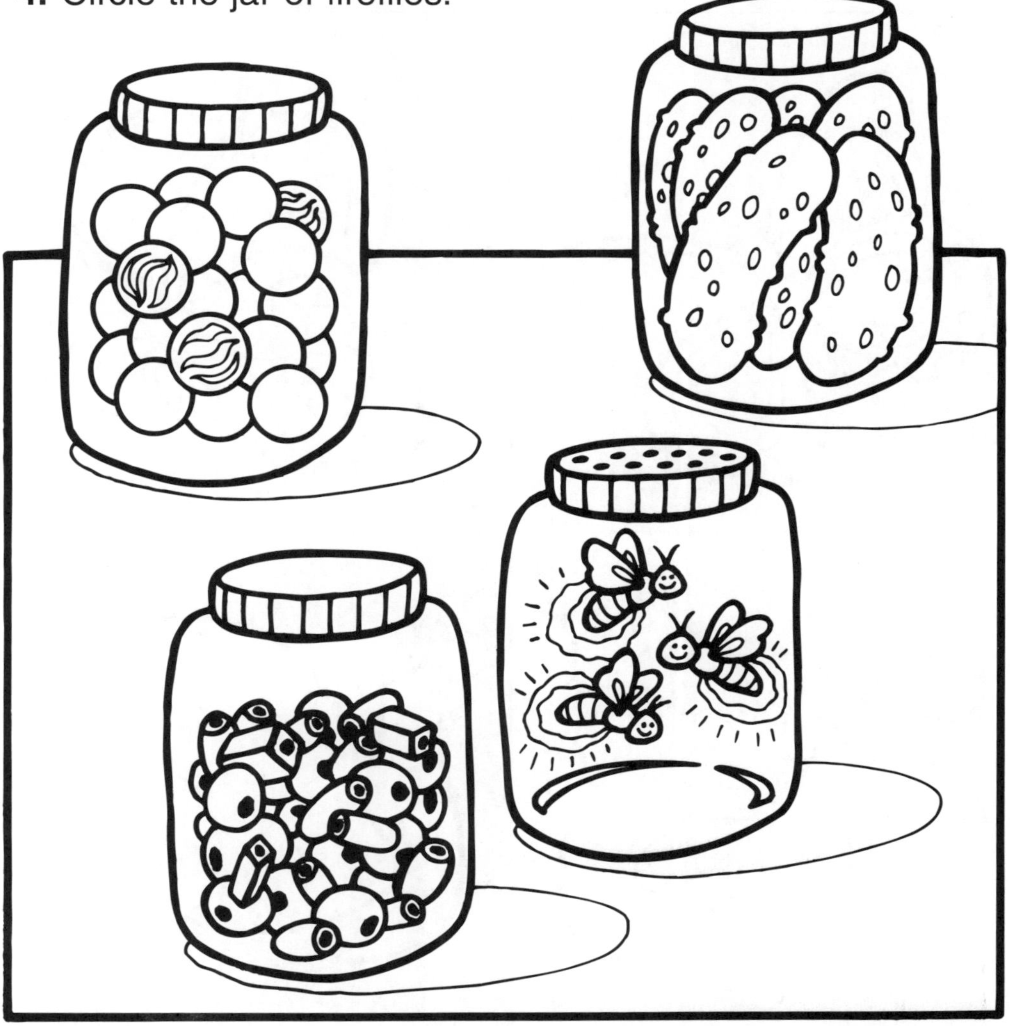

Butterflies

Directions:

1. Use a red crayon to color the butterfly that has spots on its wings.
2. Use a yellow crayon to color the butterfly that is showing its legs.

Bears

Directions:

1. Draw an **X** on the object that does not belong.
2. Use a brown crayon to color the mother and baby bear.

Around the House

Directions: Color the house green. Then do the following:

1. Use a blue crayon to circle the bathtub.
2. Use a brown crayon to add spots to the horse.
3. Use a purple crayon to color the bed.
4. Use a yellow crayon to color the baby's hair.

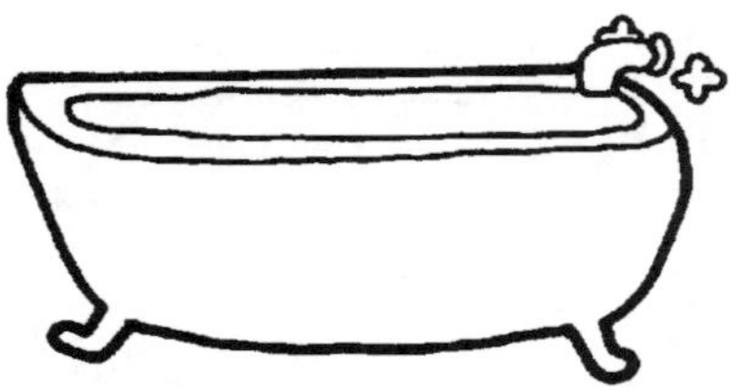

Around the Barn

Directions: Color the barn brown. Then follow these directions:

1. Use a yellow crayon to color the hay.
2. Draw a black **X** on the fireplace.
3. Color the lamb's wool pink.
4. Draw green grass under the cow's feet.

Around the Schoolhouse

Directions: Color the schoolhouse red. Then follow these directions:

1. Use a black crayon to color the train.
2. Draw a big, red **C** on the chalkboard.
3. Draw a purple circle around the desk.
4. Color the crayons green and yellow.

Draw a Ball

Directions: Follow the steps to draw a ball. After you finish Step 3, color your new ball.

1.

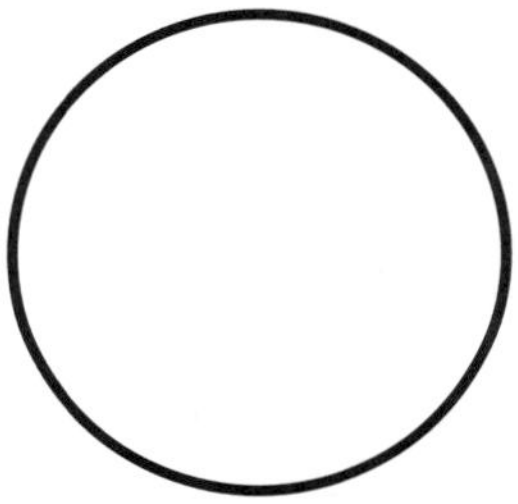

2.

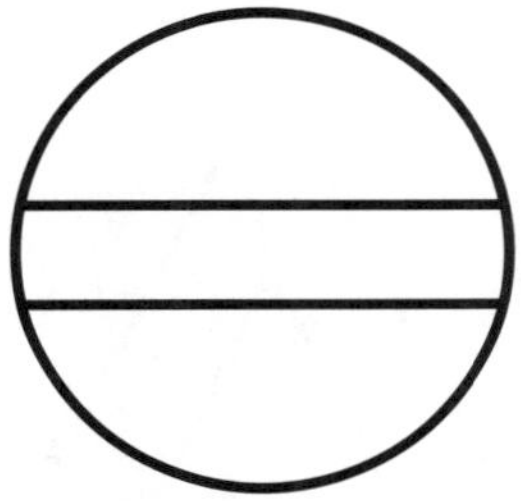

3.

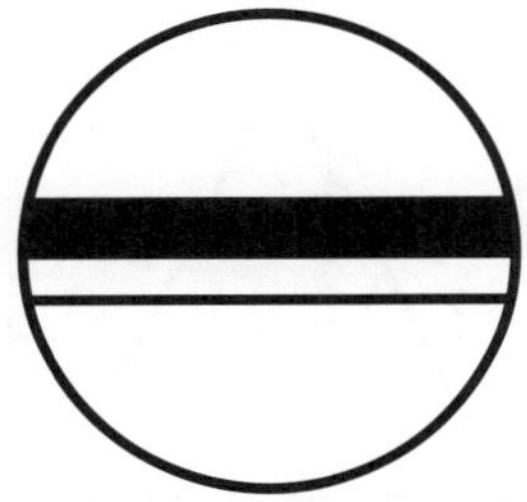

Draw a Tepee

Directions: Follow the steps to draw a tepee. After Step 3, color your new tepee.

1.

2.

3.

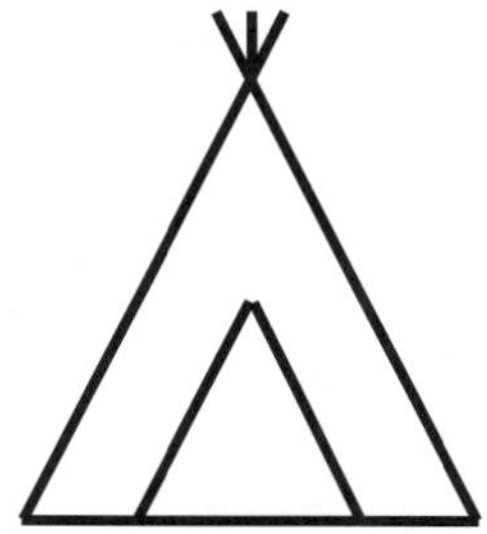

Draw a Fish

Directions: Follow the steps to draw a fish. After Step 3, color your new fish.

1.

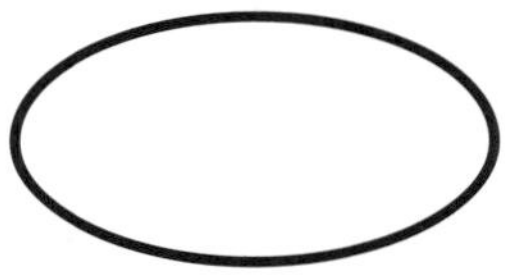

2.

3.

Under the Table

Directions:

1. Draw a ball under the table.
2. Draw a box on the table.
3. Draw a cloud over the table.
4. Draw a candy cane beside the table.

Your House

Directions:

1. Draw a doorknob on the door.
2. Draw two windows on the house.
3. Draw a bird over the house.
4. Draw a person next to the house.

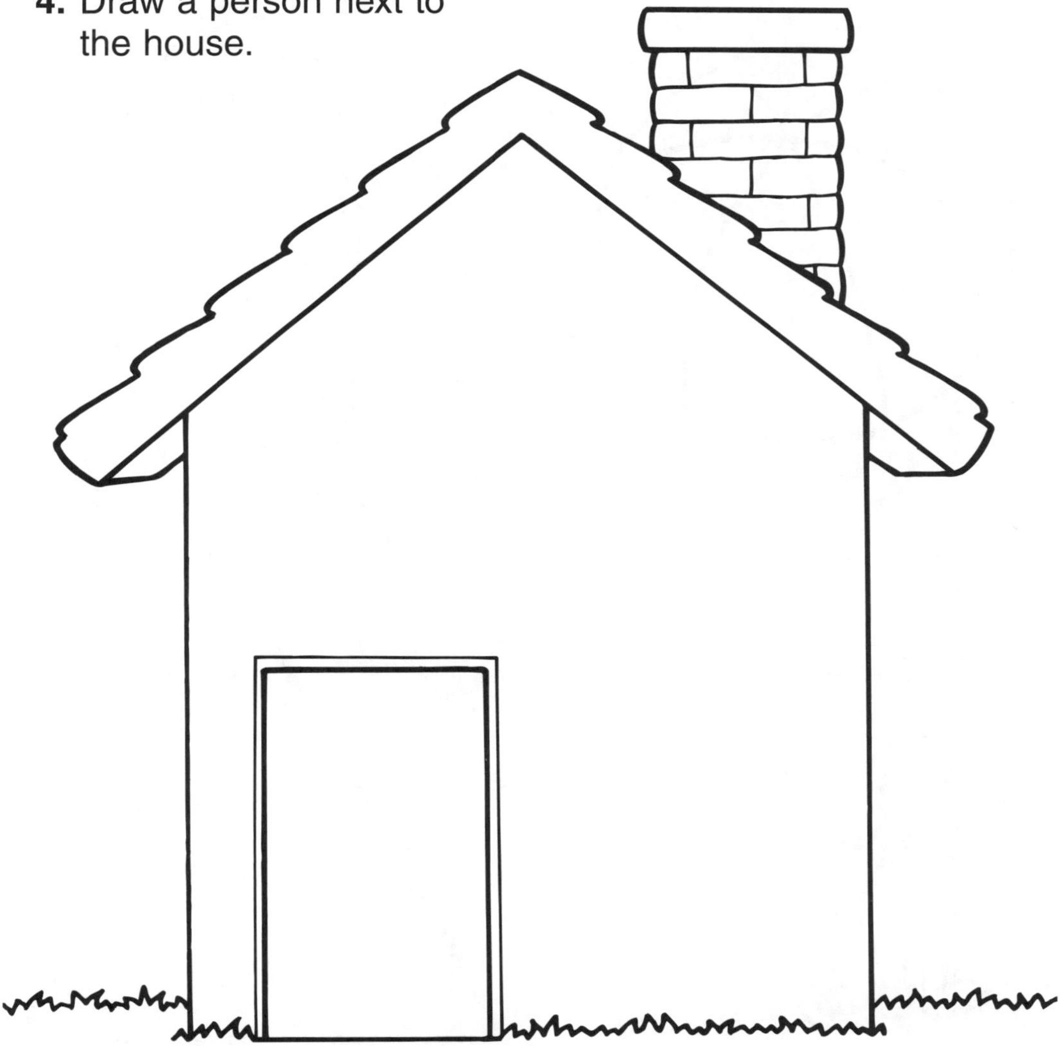

Big Dog, Little Dog

Directions:

1. Draw a line from the larger dog to the smaller dog.
2. Draw a line from the larger triangle to the smaller triangle.
3. Draw a line from the smaller ball to the larger ball.

On the Ladder

Directions:

1. Draw a circle at the top of the ladder.
2. Draw an **X** at the middle of the ladder.
3. Draw a box at the bottom of the ladder.
4. Draw a person next to the ladder.

Up and Down

Directions:

1. Draw an **X** under the person who is *up*.
2. Draw a circle around the person who is *down*.
3. Draw a sun above the picture.
4. Draw some grass at the bottom of the page.

In the Doghouse

Directions:

1. Draw a flower beside the doghouse.
2. Draw a bone below the doghouse.
3. Draw a bird above the doghouse.
4. Color the dog inside the doghouse.

Sailing Along

Directions:

1. Draw a flag at the top of the sailboat.
2. Draw a circle in the middle of the sail.
3. Draw a fish below the sailboat.
4. Draw a sun above the sailboat.

Make a Face

Directions:

1. Draw a face on the person.
2. Draw ears on the side of the head.
3. Draw a circle on one hand.
4. Draw a square on the other hand.

Singing Birds

Directions:

1. Color the two birds that look the same yellow.
2. Use a red crayon to circle the two birds that have their mouths open.
3. Use a blue crayon to draw a box around the bird that is flying.

Fish in the Sea

Directions:

1. Color the two fish that are the same.
2. Use a purple crayon to color the three fish on the left.

Color the Biggest

Directions:

1. Use a green crayon to color the biggest object in each row.
2. Use a black crayon to put an **X** on the smallest object in each row.

Circle the Smallest

Directions:

1. Use a blue crayon to circle the smallest object in each row.
2. Use a black crayon to put an **X** on the biggest object in each row.

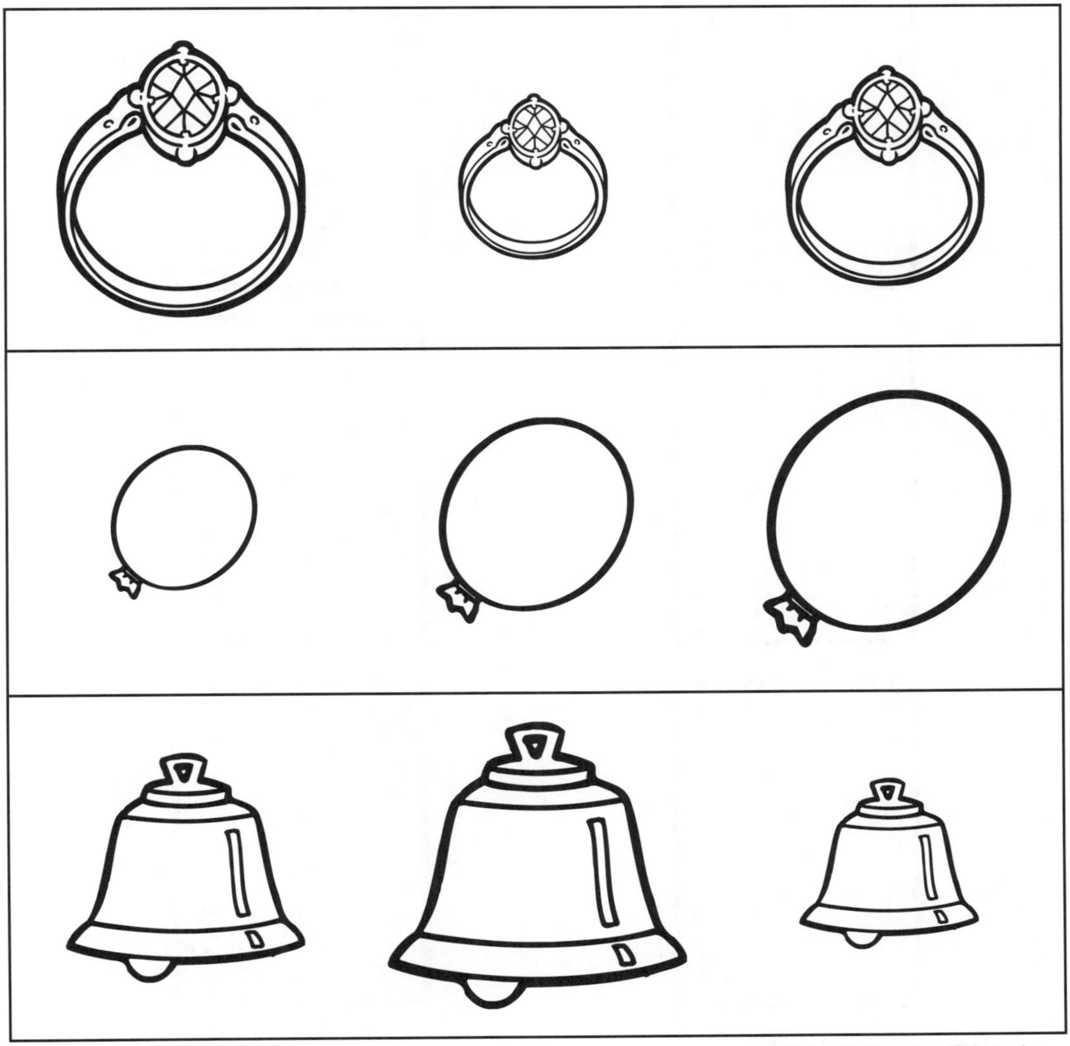

Diamonds and Hearts

Directions:

1. Use a red crayon to color all of the hearts on this page.
2. Use a yellow crayon to color all of the diamonds on this page.

Babies Everywhere

Directions:

1. Draw a red circle around the two babies that look the same.
2. Draw a blue circle around the two babies that are holding balls.
3. Draw a brown box around the baby that is on his back.

Box of Tools

Directions: Color the tools that are outside of the box.

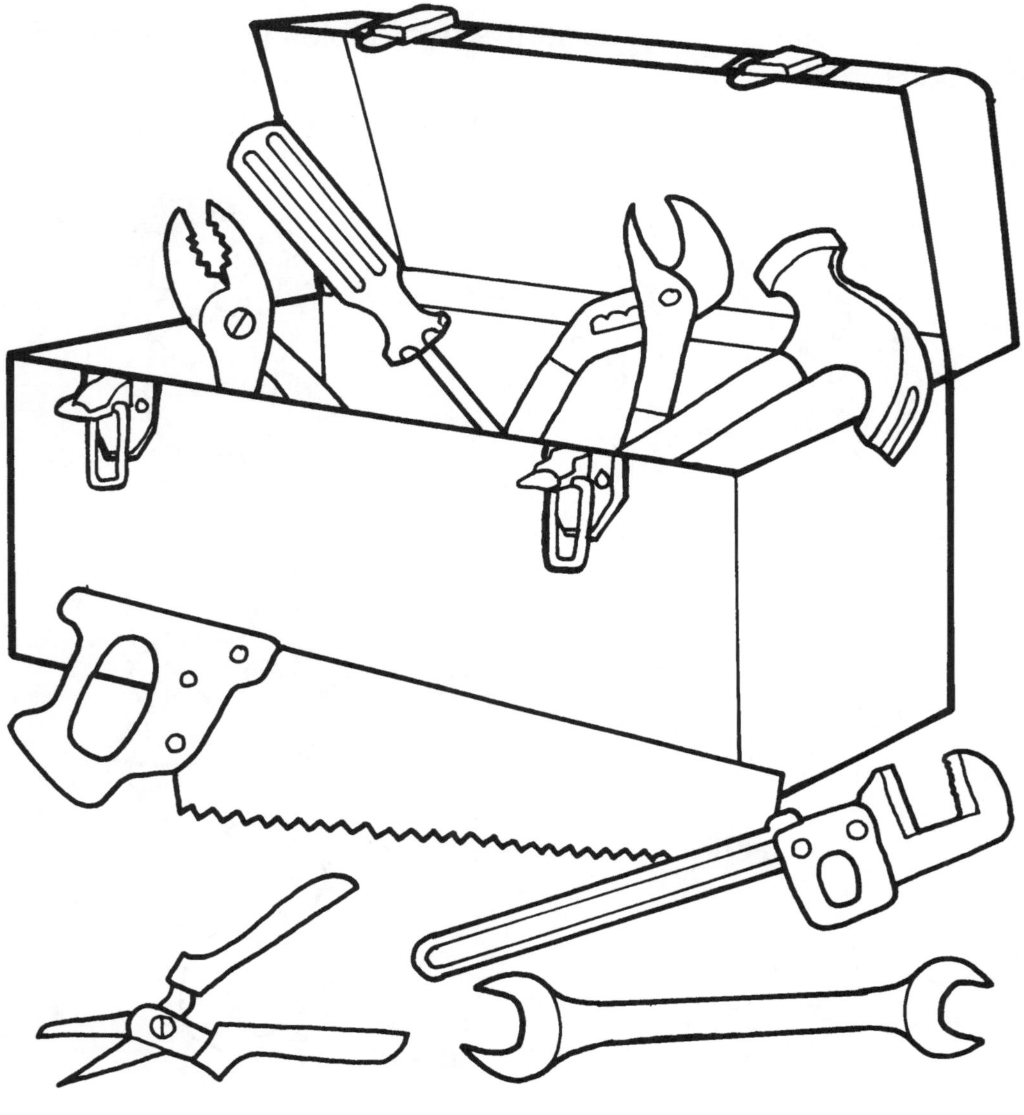

Box of Toys

Directions: Color the toys that are in the box. Draw a blue **X** on the rocking horse.

Bears in the Woods

Directions:

1. Use a brown crayon to color the bear that is near the tree.
2. Use a yellow crayon to color the bear that is far from the tree.
3. Draw a squirrel running up the tree.

Add Your Own Flag

Directions:

1. Draw a flag on each pole.
2. Draw a box on each table.
3. Draw a ball on each chair.

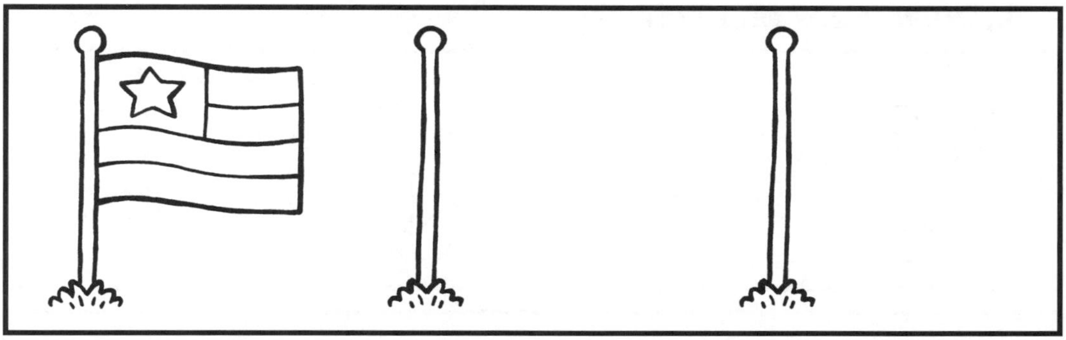

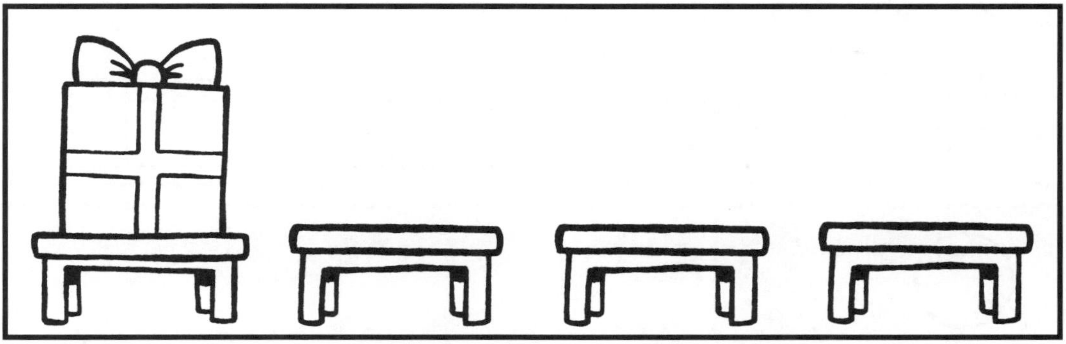

Add Your Own Flower

Directions:

1. Draw a flower on each stem.
2. Draw a roof on each house.
3. Draw a circle on each triangle.
4. Draw a box on each wagon.

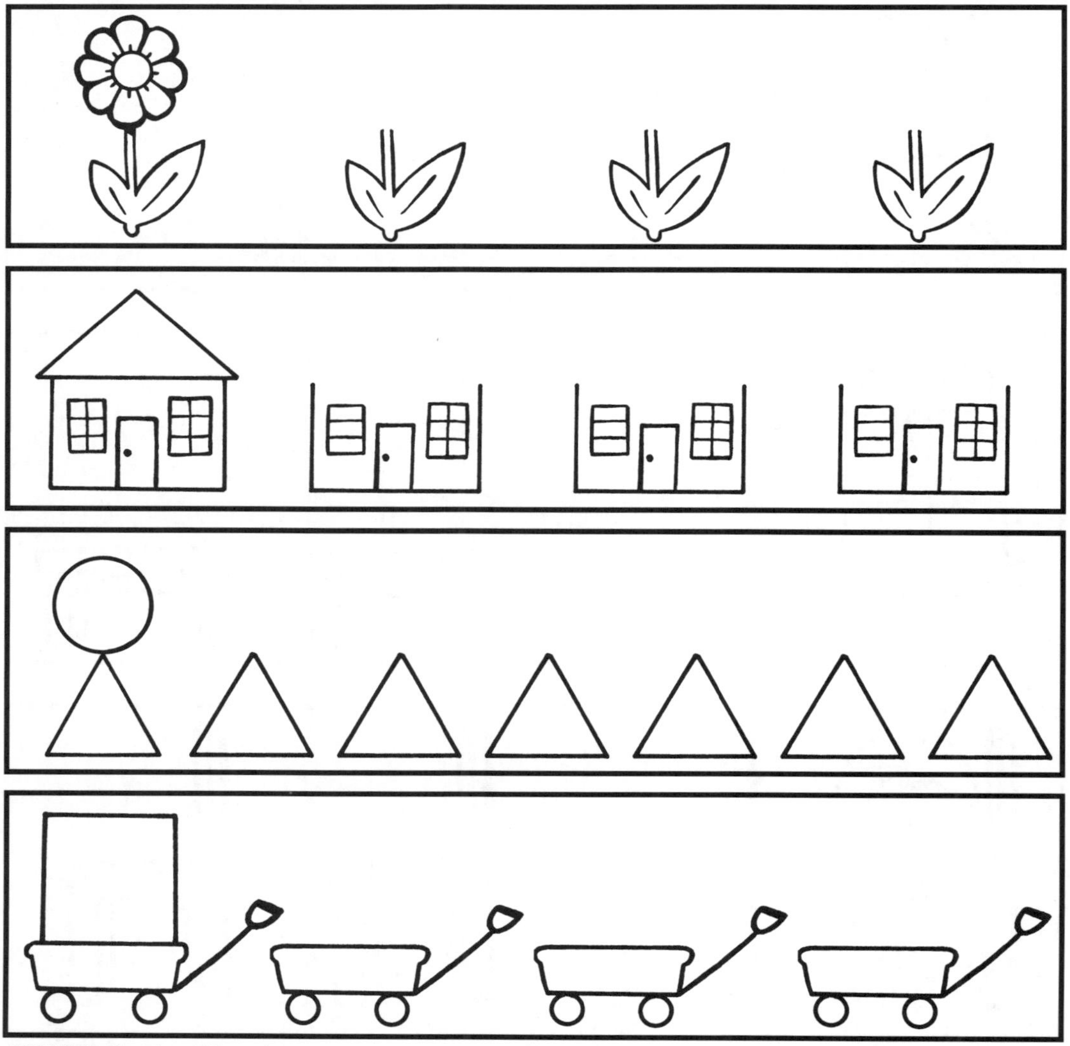

Add Your Own Chimney

Directions:

1. Draw a yolk in each egg.
2. Draw a chimney and window on each house.
3. Draw a circle around each star.
4. Draw an egg for each duck.

Beginning, Middle, and End

Directions:

- Write **1** under the picture that shows the beginning.
- Write **2** under the picture that shows the middle.
- Write **3** under the picture that shows the end.

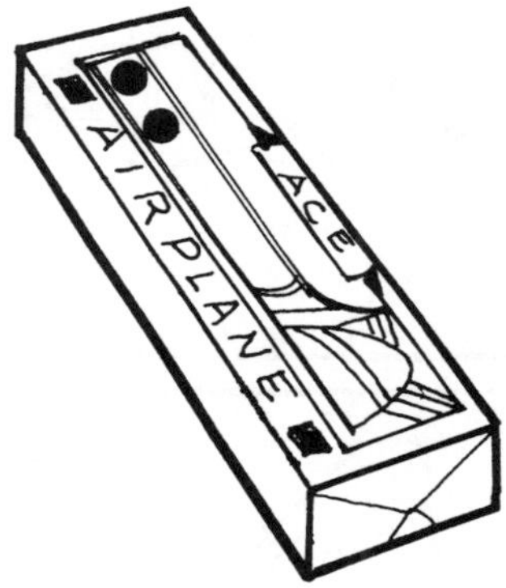

______ ______ ______

______ ______ ______

Circles and Squares

Directions:

1. Color the top circle red.
2. Color the middle circle yellow.
3. Color the bottom circle green.

1. Color the middle square purple.
2. Color the bottom square orange.
3. Color the top square blue.

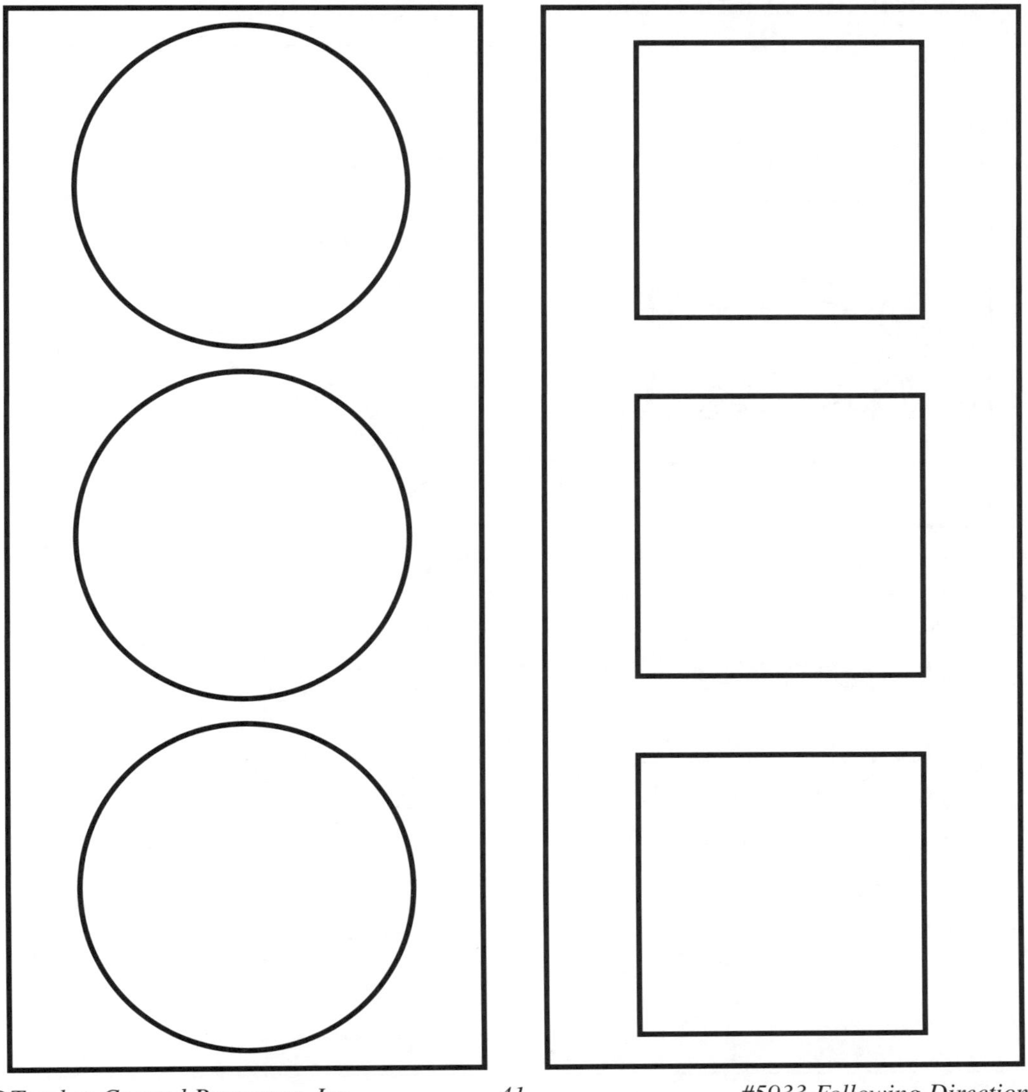

Baking a Birthday Cake

Directions:

1. Write the numbers 1, 2, 3, and 4 in the small boxes to show how to make a cake in the correct order.
2. Draw 6 candles on the cake.
3. Color the finished cake pink.

Apple Trees

Directions: Draw apples on the trees. Use the number on the tree to tell you how many apples to draw.

Firefighters

Directions: Look at the two firefighters. Follow the coloring directions.

- Color the firefighter's hair that is the *longest* yellow.
- Color the firefighter's hose that is the *shortest* brown.
- Color the firefighter's hose that is the *longest* orange.
- Color the firefighter's hose that is the *shortest* purple.

Springtime

Directions: Follow the directions to complete the picture. Color the picture.

- Draw a sun *above* the bird.
- Draw a flower *between* the trees.
- Draw a worm *under* the ground.

A Toy Shelf

Directions:

Draw . . .
- a ball between the airplane and the teddy bear.
- a rocket to the left of the car.
- a football to the right of the clown.

Color . . .
- the toys on the top shelf red.
- the toys on the middle shelf blue.
- the toys on the bottom shelf green.

Elves Are Everywhere!

Directions

1. Color the elf under the tree green.
2. Color the elf beside the flower blue.
3. Color the elf above the jump rope red.
4. Color the elf on the swing purple.

Following Directions

Directions: Follow the directions below to color the house and its surroundings.

Color the  red.

Color the  brown.

Color the  green.

Color the  yellow.

Color the 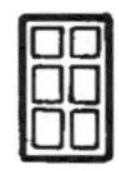 blue.

Color the  yellow.

My Shoe

Directions: Listen to my clues to figure out which shoe belongs to me.

- My shoe is not the longest. Cross out the longest shoe.
- My shoe does not have the shortest laces. Cross out the shoe with the shortest laces.
- My shoe has the highest heel. Circle my shoe.

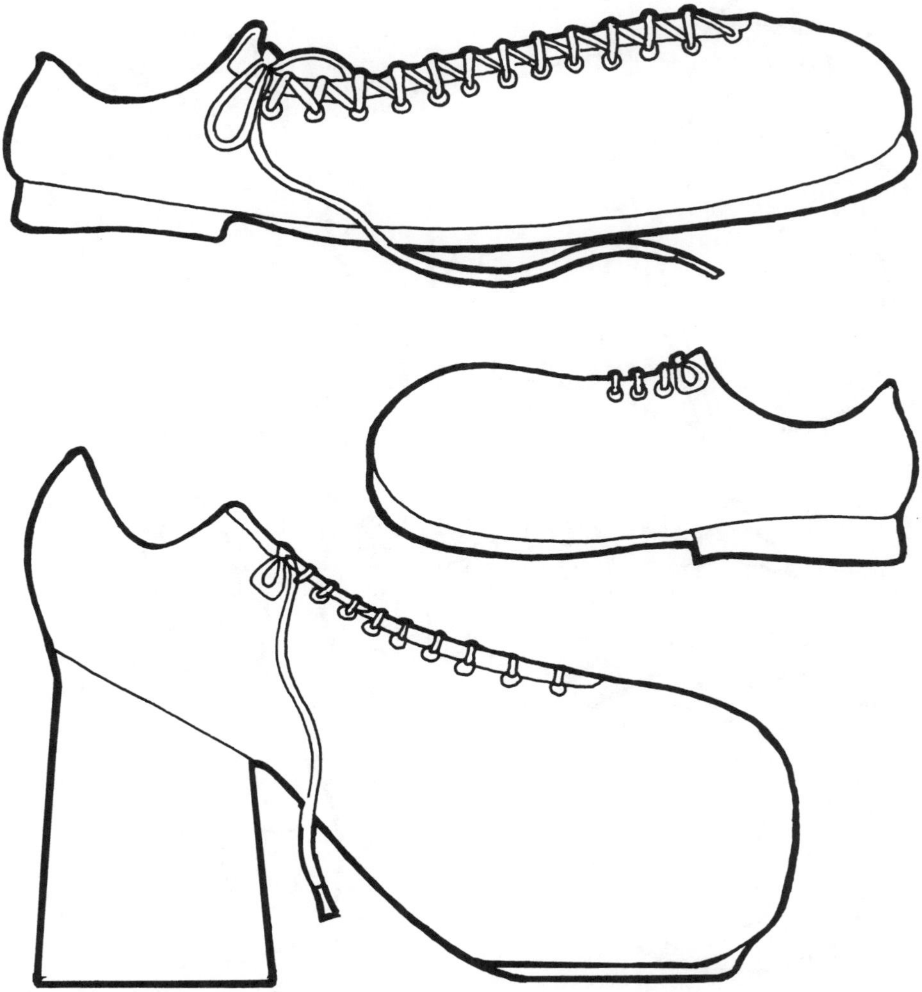

Snowman Search

Directions:

1. Find the snowman with 3 buttons. Color it red.
2. Find the snowman wearing a scarf. Color it green.
3. Find the snowman with only 2 pockets. Color it yellow.
4. Find the snowman holding a broom. Color it blue.

Shapes Bear

Directions: Color every space with a □ brown.
Color every space with a ○ blue.

Parking Lot

Directions: Color the vehicle in each row that is facing *left*. Cross out the other vehicles.

Waiting Your Turn

Directions: Draw a hat on the person in each line who is facing *right*.

Equal Sets

Directions: Count the objects in each set. Draw an equal set in the box on the right.

1. 	
2. 	
3. 	
4. 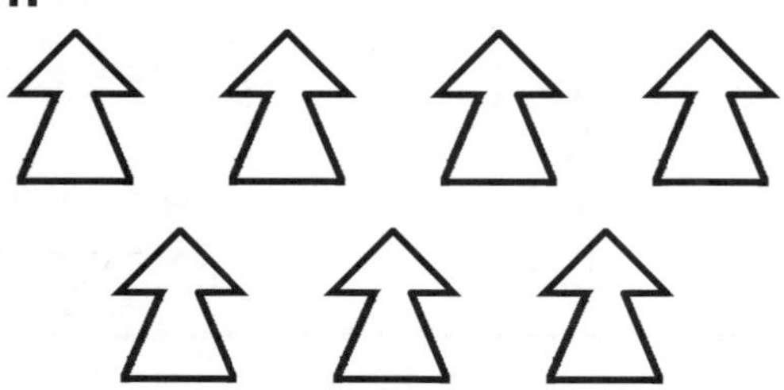	

Color the Kites

Directions: Color the kite at the top right yellow.
Color the kite on the top left red.
Color the kite on the bottom right green.
Color the kite at the bottom left blue.

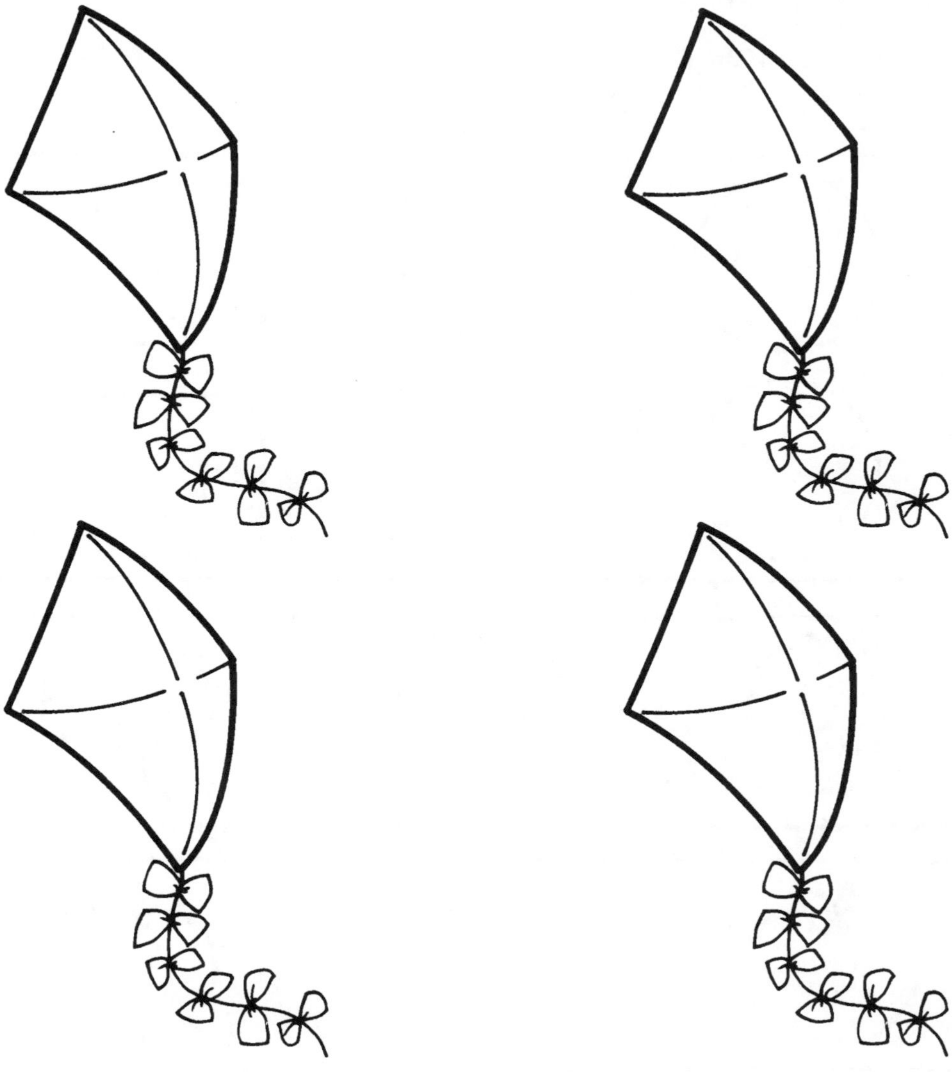

Follow the Directions

Directions:

1. Color the top circle blue.
2. Color the tree on the left green.
3. Color the middle apple yellow.
4. Color the bottom square purple.
5. Color the tree on the right brown.
6. Color the apple on the left red.

Which Way Is West?

Directions:

1. Color the ball south of the backpack yellow.
2. Color the skateboard east of the backpack red.
3. Color the ball west of the pencil orange.
4. Color the skateboard north of the pencil blue.

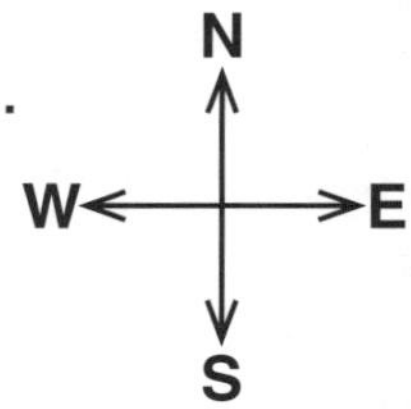

Fish Drawing Lesson

Directions: Follow the steps to draw a fish inside the box.

1. Draw a football. 
2. Add a triangle tail. 
3. Put on the eye and mouth. 
4. Add the fins. 
5. Draw the fish's scales. 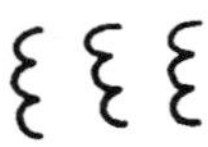
6. Now color your fish.

Does your fish look like this?

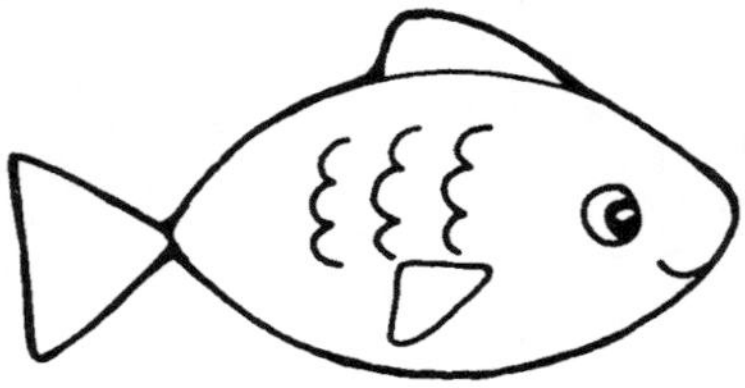

Fish Bowls

Directions: Look at the two fishbowls in each row. Follow the instructions below each set of fishbowls to add fish to the bowls.

- Draw 3 green fish in the fish bowl on the *left*.
- Draw 4 red fish in the fish bowl on the *right*.

- Draw 2 yellow fish in the fish bowl on the *left*.
- Draw 5 blue fish in the fish bowl on the *right*.

Shapes Tree

Directions: Color every space with a □ brown.
Color every space with a ○ green.
Color every space with a △ blue.

Color the Numbers

Directions: Color every space with a **1** yellow.

Color every space with a **2** green.

Color every space with a **3** blue.

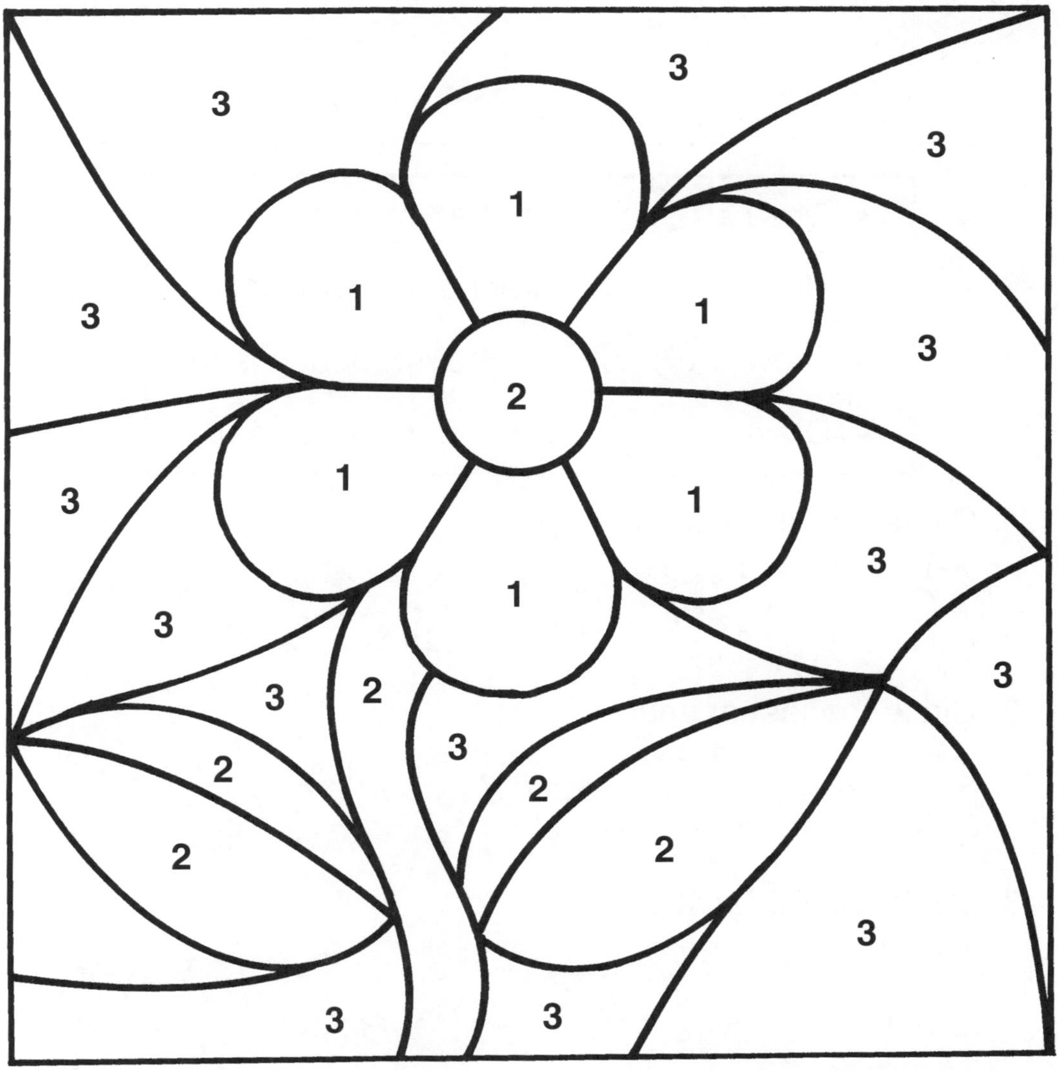

Animal Ordering

Directions: Finish numbering the bears in order. Then follow the directions in the box below.

A. 

B. 

C. 

D. 

______ st   ______ nd   ______ rd   ______ th

- Draw a 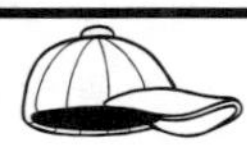 on the 3rd bear.
- Draw a  around the 1st bear.
- Draw  on the 4th bear's face.
- Draw a  around the 2nd bear.

1. Circle the 3rd animal.

2. Circle the last animal.

3. Circle the 6th animal.

This Award Is Presented To

____

for

★ Doing Your Best

★ Trying Hard

★ Not Giving Up

★ Making a Great Effort